THE GEORGIAN BAWDYHOUSE

Emily Brand

A WOMAN OF ALL TRADES,
from Covent Garden.
Published as the Act directs Octr. 20. 1781. by Turner Snow Hill

Published in Great Britain in 2012 by Shire Publications Ltd, Midland House, West Way, Botley, Oxford OX2 0PH, United Kingdom.

44-02 23rd Street, Suite 219. Long Island City, NY 11101, USA.

E-mail: shire@shirebooks.co.uk www.shirebooks.co.uk

A CIP catalogue record for this book is available from the British Library.

Shire Library no. 700.

ISBN-13: 978 0 74781 169 5

Emily Brand has asserted her right under the Copyright, Designs and Patents Act, 1988, to be identified as the author of this book.

Designed by Tony Truscott Designs, Sussex, UK and typeset in Perpetua and Gill Sans.

Printed in China through Worldprint Ltd.

12 13 14 15 16   10 9 8 7 6 5 4 3 2 1

COVER IMAGE

Plate III from *A Rake's Progress: The Rake at the Rose-Tavern* by William Hogarth (1697–1764). The inebriated Tom Rakewell has his pockets picked by a couple of prostitutes (courtesy of the Trustees of Sir John Soane's Museum, London/Bridgeman Art Library).

TITLE PAGE IMAGE

A Woman of All Trades, from Covent Garden. Anonymous print of 1782. Courtesy of the Library of Congress.

CONTENTS PAGE IMAGE

Although later distinguished as the fat 'Prince of Whales' of the Regency era, the future George IV enjoyed a reputation for sexual and fiscal profligacy from his youth. He is shown here in his early twenties, reclining in a bordello with Mother Windsor and two women of pleasure. His male companion, vomiting in a corner, is clearly not enjoying his amours overmuch.

ACKNOWLEDGEMENTS

Permissions to reproduce illustrations are gratefully acknowledged as follows:

The British Library Board, P.C.30.i.10 frontispiece, page 7 (top), 11621.e.5.(3), page 21 (top); Cheryl Leigh, page 48 (bottom left); Chetham's Library, Manchester, UK/The Bridgeman Art Library, page 51; Corbis, page 39 (bottom); The Foundling Museum, London, UK/The Bridgeman Art Library, page 13; The Lewis Walpole Library, Yale University, pages 5, 8 (bottom), 19, 23, 25 (top right), 30 (top), 32, 34 (top left), 40, 42 (bottom), 44 (top), 45 (bottom), 48 (top and bottom right), 50 and 54; Library of Congress, title page, contents page, pages 8 (top), 9 (bottom), 10 (top), 11 (top), 18, 20, 27, 28, 29 (both), 34 (bottom), 35 (bottom), 38, 39 (top), 43 (right), 44 (bottom) and 55; Museum für Verhütung und Schwangerschaftsabbruch, Vienna, pages 30 (bottom) and 37; Philip Mould Ltd, London/The Bridgeman Art Library, page 6; The Stapleton Collection/The Bridgeman Art Library, page 14 (top right); Tate Collection, page 26; The Trustees of the British Museum, pages 7 (bottom), 21 (bottom) and 49.

The remaining images are from the author's collection.

With thanks to Keri Griffiths and Ade Teal for helping me on my way through a number of historical adventures, from sod houses in the Wild West to sodomy in the Georgian navy. Thanks also to Nigel Jeffries and William A. Gordon for their kind help with images.

Dedicated to Chloe Ashton, Kasia Budner, Danny Cartridge, David Cox and Jo Sohn-Rethel. Thank you all for being such an inspiration.

CONTENTS

SHIP TAVERN

INTRODUCTION:
A FASHION FOR VICE

D URING EASTER WEEK of 1668, London was in uproar. Armed with 'iron bars, poleaxes, long staves and other weapons' and waging war with sin itself, a swarm of rioters – swelling to forty thousand according to some fevered reports – tore through the city's disreputable districts. Elements among them were frighteningly militant, dividing into regiments, nominating captains and marching behind colours. The common brothels of Moorfields and East Smithfield were devastated, but the moral crusaders also cast a narrowed eye at the profligate court of Charles II. Watching events unfold, Samuel Pepys noted that some were itching to 'go and pull down the great bawdy-house at White Hall.'

Houses of ill fame had long suffered at the hands of mobs meting out this 'ancient administration of justice'. During the seventeenth century, London apprentices routinely marked Shrovetide by raiding brothels or seeking out prostitutes and imprisoning them over Lent. While the eyebrow of the law was usually barely even raised, the Bawdyhouse Riots of 1668 resulted in fifteen men being tried for high treason, four of whom were hanged. Clearly, appropriating the brothel as a political symbol was a dangerous venture.

Despite these outbreaks of popular protest, the 'long' eighteenth century – from the coronation of Charles II in 1660 to the death of the equally debauched George IV in 1830 – is often perceived as a high point of sexual liberation in England. The Restoration era persists in the popular imagination as one ruled by passions. Even the Archbishop of Canterbury was described as 'as very a wencher as can be', and the Bishop of Rochester once found himself in hot water for putting his hand down a gentleman's codpiece at the dinner table. Erotic paraphernalia and libertine literature were celebrated in the drinking clubs and sex societies that took root around the country, and the walls of public taverns were embellished with pornographic images.

The Georgians, therefore, considered themselves well acquainted with sex, and gloried in their inheritance. However, over the course of the eighteenth century old assumptions about sexual matters were scrutinised as the nation

Opposite:
Portsmouth Point (1814). Thomas Rowlandson was renowned for his salacious images, and he must have relished devising this harbour scene. Sailors made the most of any opportunity to carouse with willing women, as those in and about the Ship Tavern here demonstrate.

Nell Gwynne, by Sir Peter Lely, c. 1670s. From a background of poverty and debauchery, she rose to become a renowned comic actress and Charles II's most popularly beloved mistress (she teasingly referred to him as 'Charles III', because he was her third lover of that name).

Opposite, bottom: The eighteenth century continues to be perceived as an era of sexual liberation and rampant promiscuity. Here, a group of harlots and rakes – in various states of undress – sing lustily, waving their hats above their heads as an intoxicated bawd snores in the corner. (A Sketch From Nature, 1784).

crept towards modern understandings of gender and reproduction. Sexual myths – including the possibility of spontaneous sex changes, amorous embraces reviving the dead, and sexual position determining a child's gender – faltered in the wake of scientific and anatomical research illustrating the innate differences between men and women. Amid national anxiety about a population eroded by war and the growing idealisation of the family unit, the procreative purpose of sex was re-emphasised. However, entrepreneurs and quack doctors continued to profit from the business of pleasure; an early modern precursor to Viagra, 'Viper-Wine', allowed 'gray-bearded gallants' to 'feele youthfull flames agin', and rudimentary condoms became increasingly widely available.

In 1776, clergyman William Dodd chastised his country for wallowing in an age when 'vice is become fashionable, and that of Lewdness especially treated with smiles' (he was himself executed for forgery the following year). With the blossoming of print culture came the keen demand for and cheap supply of popular pornography; England was titillated by explicit engravings of varying sophistication and, with the birth of the novel, the erotic exploits of fictional whores such as Defoe's Moll Flanders and Cleland's Fanny Hill. Courtesans' memoirs were devoured by a public increasingly obsessed with scandal and 'celebrity'. The nation was openly intrigued by its sexual underworld, but perpetually troubled by the potential corruptive influence of those lurking in it. High-class prostitutes were celebrated as 'Toasts of the Town', but whispers of 'Jezebel Clubs' conspiring to manipulate the MPs they entertained reveal popular anxiety about their place in the shadows of governmental affairs. Some bawds enjoyed the patronage of the nation's most powerful men, even exerting political influence: Mother Creswell, for example, funded her lover's support of the illegitimate Duke of Monmouth's claim to the throne in the 1680s.

The culture of commercial sex was also firmly entrenched in Georgian London. In 1758, magistrate Saunders Welch lamented: 'bawdy-houses are kept in such an open and public manner [that] a stranger would think ... the whole

Left: As print
culture blossomed,
erotica followed
suit. This print
shows a group
of ladies intrigued
by a selection of
phallic objects,
possibly
rudimentary sex
toys. One woman
in Georgian
London reportedly
sold such 'widow's
comforters' on the
streets, disguising
them as children's
dolls.

7

A New Cock Wanted (1810). Illustrating the Georgians' bawdy sense of humour, this print shows a historical precedence for innuendos about handsome plumbers.

Madams and whores regularly featured in political prints, usually to dishonour the gentlemen consorting with them. Here, however, the Duke of Wellington (right) and the Earl of Eldon are cast as brawling Oxford bawds. (*Sketch of a Row in Parliament Street, c. 1829*).

town was one general stew.' To some, the city's economy seemed frighteningly dependent on the industry; one German visitor postulated that if it collapsed 'the fine arts would be frightened away; one half of the inhabitants would be deprived of subsistence.' Country girls flocking to the city hoping for a change in fortunes were notoriously vulnerable and regarded as 'a sacrifice to the metropolis, offered by the thirty-nine counties'; when planning one of her own excursions to the capital, a young Jane Austen joked to her sister that she would inevitably 'fall a Sacrifice to the arts of some fat Woman who would make me drunk with small Beer.'

Naturally, vice was not confined to the capital. Port towns embraced demobilised sailors to their bosom (one euphemism for a whore was one who had 'studied natural philosophy at the University of Portsmouth') and bawdyhouses flourished in fashionable resorts such as Bath and Brighton. In 1796, a Brighton tourist guide described its town as 'where the sinews of

morality are so happily relaxed, that a bawd and a baroness may snore in the same tenement.' Residents of Oxford grumbled that 'Pimps abus'd both Church and College', and the whole of Exeter and Devon was infested by harlotry 'to a most lamentable degree'. Newspapers in Edinburgh, Dublin, Norwich, York and Bristol all hungrily detailed the arrests and misdeeds of their local whores, bawds and libertines.

Popular attitudes towards women making a living 'trading on their own bottom' also evolved as the

William Hogarth was prominent among a number of notables whose work drew attention to the plight of prostitutes during the mid-1700s. His series of engravings titled *A Harlot's Progress* enjoyed huge commercial success, and he was a generous donor to London's Foundling Hospital, which housed unwanted or illegitimate infants.

nation nurtured changed ideas about public charity, womanhood and marriage. It was popularly believed that the rabble of harlots plying their trade in the 1600s did so simply because they were sexually insatiable. No doubt playing to male fantasies, others were allegedly fallen gentlewomen, victims of the Civil War now willing to 'master your *Britches* and take all your *Riches*'; one even identifed herself as 'Lady Mary Tudor', a nymphomaniac daughter of Charles II and Moll Davis.

The Merry Accident, c. 1759. Some courtesans enjoyed celebrity status. When Kitty Fisher fell (or wantonly threw herself) from her horse in St James's Park in March 1759, reports of her skirts in disarray, and her pretty thighs exposed, featured in almost every London paper.

Right: *Harmony Before Matrimony* (1805). Satirising the relationship between the sexes, this James Gillray print portrays a couple apparently in the throes of a beautiful romance. The brawling, squawking cats beside them hint at the future that truly awaits them in marriage.

Opposite, top: *Lodgings to Let* (1814). A man enquires after lodgings, hoping that a little more might be thrown into the bargain. Men of pleasure often presumed that the favours of even genteel ladies could be 'bought' for the right price.

Opposite, bottom: Plate III of Hogarth's *A Harlot's Progress* (1732). The heroine, Moll Hackabout, is already slipping from fortune's favour, and reclines in a common garret. Her tragic fall from grace and ultimate death unraveled over a series of six prints.

When public philanthropy became a fashionable pursuit in the mid-eighteenth century, reformers portrayed prostitutes as figures deserving pity; as Moll Flanders explained, 'Vice came in always at the Door of Necessity, not at the Door of Inclination.' As marital fidelity became somewhat romanticised towards the close of the century, however, they were recast as a social evil, and as attitudes towards prostitutes shifted, so did the opportunities available to them.

The cause of women's rights was as yet little more than a low murmur, and the perception of women as a commodity was reinforced by the legal status of wives as their husbands' property. In a culture less obsessed than ours with the ideal of 'love' and generally derisive of female intellectual autonomy, viewing women as property in a fiscal and a sexual sense was conventional. The wife, mistress, courtesan and whore: all were defined in relation to men, and all were, in some sense, depicted in the milieu of commercial transaction, as Henry Fielding's equation of marriage with legal prostitution and Defoe's tract on 'matrimonial whoredom' indicate. For sexually active women, there was a fine line between virtue and vice, and it was generally assumed that the body of almost any woman could be bought, for the right price.

But while common harlots openly sold their favours, what of kept mistresses, or servants seduced by promises and fine trinkets? Although she earned a wage winding silk, Elizabeth Hammond accepted a silver watch after lying with an acquaintance in 1754. Did seizing an opportunity, just once, make her a whore? Difficulties in defining the prostitute extend to generalisations about the brothel. Landlords might turn a blind eye to what happened under their roof, or perhaps seek to benefit from it. In the 1790s, for example, Jonathan Britt charged his lodgers weekly board, adding 2s for every man who accompanied them home. Lodging houses, bath-houses (or *bagnios*), and taverns: all were used for illicit rendezvous, but not all exclusively so.

However, houses given over entirely to the pursuit of pleasure did exist – from grimy garrets to 'Mansions of Lewdness and Obscenity' – and they present something of a paradox. They were homes, and places of work; places to satisfy the most exotic lusts, or be caught in the most compromising situations. They represented sinful depravity, yet bred up some of the most celebrated beauties of the age, and were frequented by England's most illustrious gentlemen. These establishments were facetiously referred to as 'nunneries' or 'Schools of Venus', and sometimes defined the character of entire districts, such as London's Covent Garden or Avon Street in Bath. The Georgian bawdyhouse stood outside the realm of respectability, and yet the many social and ideological transformations of the era were crucial in shaping how it was perceived and what went on within its walls.

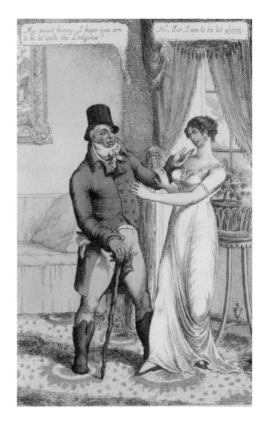

THE BAWD AND HER HOUSEHOLD

O N ONE JAUNT TO THE CAPITAL, Sir Charles Hanbury Williams found himself confronted with the renowned 'Mother' Douglas (an ironic epithet bestowed upon mature female brothel-keepers), and he later described her as 'a great flabby stinking swearing hollowing ranting Billingsgate Bawd'. In fact, Jane Douglas was relatively well liked, but the popular stereotype of the corpulent, grimacing – and in Elizabeth Creswell's case, occasionally bearded – procuress was already well established in the public imagination by the 1700s. They had reigned over the sex industry for centuries, and London's bawds – or 'keepers of the house', as they preferred to term themselves – enjoyed no inconsiderable measure of notoriety.

Mother Holland filled her Elizabethan Bankside establishment with 'petulant, paynted and half-gilded girls', and protected her property with a moat and drawbridge. The half-mythical 'Long Meg of Westminster' – reputedly 7 feet tall, with a prize-fighter's physique – 'kept alwaies twenty courtizans in her house', and folklore attests that she was laid to rest in Westminster Abbey. With Cromwell and almost all enthusiasm for his Puritan regime laid to rest, Restoration England crawled with madams laying claim to splendid establishments and the most beautiful girls. Mother Creswell was particularly proud of her brood, 'from the cole-black blyng-fast to the golden-lock'd insatiate'. Perhaps hoping to give depth to the facetious conflation of brothels with 'nunneries' and brothel-keepers with 'abbesses', Elizabeth Wisebourne – the greatest bawd of Queen Anne's reign – adopted an aspect of deep piety, and kept an open Bible in the hallway of her house.

In reality, their stories were more diverse than the pock-marked crones of popular caricatures suggested. In 1705, *The London-Bawd* defined its eponymous heroine as 'the Refuse of an Old Whore, who having been burnt herself, does like Charcoal help to set greener Wood on Fire', and bawdry was indeed a logical career move for prostitutes whose star was growing dim. However, surveys of London brothels indicate that it was not unusual to find brothel-keepers who were not yet twenty-five. Some, such as Charlotte Hayes – the manageress of one of the most glamorous stews of the

Opposite: Detail from Hogarth's *March of the Guards to Finchley* (1750). Peering through the open windows of Mother Douglas's house in Covent Garden, we see her in an attitude of prayer while her girls beckon to passing soldiers. The cats on the roof (long associated with brothels or 'catteries') and the 'Charles II' tavern sign hint at its status of ill repute.

Above: Former prostitute and bawd Moll King. After her husband's death, she assumed sole management of King's Coffeehouse. She was indicted as many as twenty times for keeping disorderly houses, and admonished her rivals for tyrannical treatment of their girls.

Above right: Mother Holland's Bankside brothel, known as 'Holland's Leaguer', is described in this seventeenth-century engraving as filled with 'dainty Devils drest in humane Shape'.

Right: This detail from Plate I of *A Harlot's Progress* shows the infamous Mother Needham luring the fresh-faced rustic innocent Moll straight from the York coach into her house. Her brothel, The Old Bell, can be seen in the background.

late eighteenth century – were raised in the houses managed by their mothers. Although female bawds were the most popularly reviled and, interestingly, more harshly punished, the business was not an exclusively feminine one: contemporary court records uncover a number of male brothel-keepers (known as 'panders') and husband-and-wife partnerships.

Regardless of the owner's professional history or personal attributes, the skilful direction of a brothel could be highly lucrative. In 1743, the *Gentleman's Magazine* speculated that by her death Mother Hayward was worth £10,000 – something approaching £1,000,000 today. The aspiring bawd's first decision: what sort of establishment did she or he intend to run? The term 'bawdyhouse' could be applied to warrens of dimly lit garrets or palatial townhouses, those trading discreetly behind sham shop-fronts and even a floating 'Scotch brothel' on the Thames known as *The Folly*.

It was an easy trade to coordinate in urban areas crippled by poverty. Londoners feared – not altogether groundlessly – that bawds prowled wagon stations and even established fake schools to ensnare innocent girls into a life of debauchery. However, these opportunities were far from just an urban phenomenon: in 1829, for example, Ann Jackson was incarcerated for 'wickedly enticing' a fifteen-year-old girl from her parents at Bradford Fair.

Tom King's coffeehouse can be seen in the detail of Hogarth's *Morning*. Tom promoted female promiscuity and his house was notorious for bringing whores and rakes together. A drunken fracas is already in full swing at 7 a.m., and fornicating couples litter the entrance.

The Oakland Cottages. Cheltenham or Fox Hunters & their Favourites.

Taken from *The English Spy* (1826), this Robert Cruickshank print gives a cheeky nod towards the ancillary country pursuits of the English gentleman; at the 'snug convent' at Oakland Cottages in Cheltenham, 'the lady abbess and the fair sisters of Cytherea perform their midnight mysteries'.

While the provincial towns and rural pockets of England were less likely to contain buildings whose income came exclusively from prostitution, public taverns and private lodgings provided ample opportunity for casual encounters.

Although prostitution itself was not illegal, harsh punishments could be brought down on 'disorderly houses' that disturbed the peace. As such, maintaining a respectable appearance was often the key to success. Many brothels and bagnios were disguised behind a façade of normality, stereotypically being dressed as a shop supplying coffee, chocolate, oysters or millinery. Indeed, some proprietors *did* pursue supplementary employment: while running a string of establishments on New Street in London, a Mr Dancer also earned a wage as clerk of nearby Bedford Chapel. When Ann Drury was accused of keeping a 'common notorious Bawdyhouse' in 1735, neighbours affirmed that they had purchased 'their Bread honestly at her House', and 'she has dealt with me for Oranges and Lemons'. History doesn't record whether Ann was the victim of slander, or simply skilled in concealing her true vocation, but it is reasonable to assume that, in reality, some lower-class brothels undertook additional commerce, whether to create the illusion of respectability or simply to sustain domestic economy.

Conversely, the protection of wealthy patrons allowed fashionable establishments to work openly. A resident of St James's, Philip Ryan, revealed

Bagnios were unabashed in advertising their trade; two such signs can be seen here in Hogarth's *Night* (1736). Also featured are trade signs depicting bunches of grapes, indicating the Bacchanalian nature of the establishments.

that the girls of a nearby house 'lolled out of the windows' to 'beckon to young men as they pass' and that their transactions were concluded before open windows, in full view of the neighbourhood. The bawd half-heartedly attempted to avoid scandal by professing to be married, 'but to all appearance, she is manager of the house.'

Entrepreneurial brothel-keepers with opportunities for financial speculation could also raise their profile by staging themed amatory entertainments. In the 1770s, as the popular imagination was captivated by the eroticism of foreign cultures revealed by the voyages of Captain Cook, Charlotte Hayes organised a Tahitian orgy, allegedly attended by twenty-three men of pleasure, 'chiefly of the first nobility', including eleven Members of Parliament.

Only a minority of bawds could aspire to elegance and riches, but stews of all ranks could boost their custom by providing specialist services. Some catered for those with fetishes including flagellation or strangulation: Theresa Berkeley's Regency whipping parlour was considered exemplary and boasted a bewildering array of equipment, including birch rods, leather straps, green nettles and a 'hook and pulley attached to the ceiling by which she could draw a man up by the hands'. Others encouraged role-play: on one occasion the *Covent Garden Journal* gleefully reported that a recent brothel raid had revealed a local tradesman's penchant for dressing as a priest. In 1775, Lord Pembroke told James Boswell of an expensive

The slogan of this satirical print (c. 1708) – 'Keep a Shop for Countenance, Kiss with Beaus for Maintenance' – indicates the strength of the contemporary association between millinery and prostitution. Some believed that exposure to fine clothing bred vanity, eventually impelling women to sell their bodies to afford material goods.

establishment staffed entirely by black women, and others claimed unrivalled talents in particular services, such as fellatio. However, all households could benefit from being prepared for less conventional requests: in 1754, when a gentleman asked prostitute Grace Riley to give him a whipping, she was obliged to scurry down to the kitchen and borrow a whisk. 'Mollyhouses' – meeting places for homosexual intercourse – also existed in urban areas, although as money was not usually involved, these should be viewed as part of a sexual subculture rather than an industry. Bath-houses may have originated as places to restore health, but by the Georgian era they were strongly associated with prostitution: one anonymous pamphlet of 1756 blasted the bagnio as 'no more than a tolerated bawdyhouse'. Serial womaniser Giacomo Casanova relished his experience at a London bagnio, a place where 'a man can sup, bathe and sleep with a fashionable courtesan' – overall, a 'magnificent debauch'.

Fears about child prostitution – and establishments profiting entirely from this industry – were rife. Certainly, many bawds felt no qualms about recruiting the very young, or propagating the myth that sleeping with a virgin would cure venereal disease. In 1822, Mary Mathews was indicted for keeping a 'brothel, of the very worst description' in Brighton. Several of her girls were under fourteen, and one only eleven years old. Elizabeth Keep's 'Temple of Aurora' specialised in girls between twelve and sixteen, although they were only to be admired (at least, that's what she said). Although it is likely that reformers exaggerated the prevalence of such houses, countless horrified contemporaries attested to girls as young as nine soliciting on the streets.

Whatever manner of house she chose to keep, no bawd could manage a successful business without the necessary tools of the trade. Furniture, medicines, contraceptives, gally-pots and phials, alcohol, foodstuffs, kitchen utensils, specialist equipment and erotic paraphernalia were all valuable

Opposite:
A Morning Ramble, or the milliner's shop (1782). A gentleman thrills two milliner's employees by offering them masquerade tickets, while his companion leans promiscuously towards another.

19

Opposite, top:
The 'Billingsgate
language' of
whores and bawds
was notoriously
foul and they had
no pretensions to
grandeur (c. 1760,
from *The New Art
and Mystery of
Gossiping*).

acquistions. In 1752, the inventory of Elizabeth Haddock's bagnio indicates relatively luxurious surroundings: it was bedecked with mahogany furniture, decorative prints, feather beds, and a stash of alcohol – including '90 gallons of arrack, 24 gallons of white wine port [and] 18 gallons of rum' – valued at almost £15,000 in modern currency. Remedial stores were essential for preserving health and for practising the trickeries necessary to keep profits from dipping. Offering a girl's virginity usually elicited the highest bids, and many prostitutes 'lost' theirs on numerous occasions; Charlotte Hayes remarked mysteriously that a maidenhead was 'as easily made as a pudding'.

Neither could a brothel be managed without staff. Servants darted through the corridors and kitchens, usually girls being groomed to enter the house's primary service or perhaps the children of the bawd or the whores. Many brothel-keepers could protect their homes quite admirably: when a quarrel arose in a Blackfriars brothel in 1763, 'the old Bawd' promptly gave the troublesome client 'a violent Blow on the Head with a Poker'. However, most establishments employed male 'bullies' to deter unwelcome intruders and assist in depriving clients of their purses.

All who were drawn into this world of vice found it difficult to escape. In 1752, within a few months of becoming a 'Protector to a House of ill Fame', William Baldwin fell from his respectable carpenter's trade to execution for assault. The fallen women themselves enjoyed no privileges.

Moralists viewed
flagellation as
a vice brought
over from the
debauched French,
and as a resort of
elderly men unable
to enjoy other
sexual pleasures.
This print of 1752,
however, portrays
a relatively young
man clearly
enjoying being
whipped with
birch rods.

The honeyed promises of the procuress were rarely realised, and having taken a girl under her wing, a shrewd bawd employed every means possible to keep her trapped there.

Below: *The Tar's Triumph* depicts the ransacking of Peter Wood's brothel, The Star, during the Sailors' Riots of 1749, and reveals much about the perceived contents of London's brothels. Medicines, gally-pots, and cosmetic aids are strewn across the streets, as their fine furniture and pornographic literature burns.

THE FALLEN WOMAN

Some there are, who are of Opinion, that to be a Woman of Pleasure is to be a Giant of Mischief.

Anonymous, *The Genuine History of Mrs Sarah Prydden* (1723)

EIGHTEENTH-CENTURY ENGLAND devised a glut of terms for its prostitutes. Some were regional – 'drazil-drozzle' in Hampshire, 'dolly-tripe' in Warwickshire – but most identified a woman's place in the hierarchy of whoredom. Clinging to the lowest rungs of the ladder were the 'bunters' and the 'hedge-whores' (the latter bestowing her favours 'on the wayside, under a hedge'); enjoying loftier heights were the 'squirrels' and 'demi-reps'. Unabashed philanderer James Boswell was enthralled by the wares on offer, 'from the splendid Madam of fifty guineas a night, down to the civil nymph with white-thread stockings', who required only a pint of wine and a shilling. But whether they stalked the streets or awaited custom in a luxury bordello, whether represented as repulsive wretches or beautiful nymphs, all were common property, all were fallen women, 'like a dirty table-cloth', to echo Boswell's uncharitable musings.

Their circumstances were as varied as their fortunes. The average age of a London whore was between sixteen and twenty-four; one figure in *Harris' List of Covent Garden Ladies* – an annually updated directory of the city's prostitutes published between 1757 and 1795 – was 'rather in the wane, having seen at least twenty-eight summers'. Those unable to boast youth and beauty worked by moonlight; one German visitor noted with horror that, towards midnight, 'the old wretches, of fifty or sixty years of age, descend from their garrets, and attack the intoxicated passengers'. Court records suggest they were as likely to be married as single; most were presumed to have allied themselves to thieves, but in reality many turned to the streets to provide for their families. To avoid detection, disassociate themselves from their family, show devotion to a lover or simply to gain renown, many adopted aliases of varying plausibility, from

Opposite:
The slatternly accommodation of a lower-class prostitute in the notorious district of London's St Giles. The smiling wench has adorned her room with broadsides of the execution of Tyburn heroes and a bunch of flowers in a chamberpot (*A St Giles's Beauty*, 1784).

the inoffensive Betsy Careless to the suggestive Poll Nimblewrist and the obscene Rosamund Sugarc—t.

Only a fortunate minority enjoyed the life of a courtesan, and their star was not always in the ascendant for long. Nevertheless, it was an old observation that 'some of the finest women in England are those, who go under the denomination of ladies of easy virtue.' Their career usually began with an invitation to join a bawd's high-class house, and her launch into lascivious society. Once brought to popular notice, their beauty inspired the era's most distinguished artists and earned them a pass into the highest circles. Flitting between illustrious lovers, they made 'guest' appearances at high-class brothels during dry spells to advertise their availability.

Those hoping to enchant powerful gentlemen required the necessary accomplishments, and were expected to perfect the arts of lewdness and gentility with equal aplomb. Madams or liveried servants escorted them into town; Miss Ledger of Mayfair was frequently seen attended by a foot-boy carrying her lap-dog on a crimson cushion. Praised by clients for having 'refine[d] our amorous amusements', girls at Jane Goadby's practised music and embroidery daily.

Despite this affected elegance, they did not necessarily hail from aristocratic backgrounds, and those plucked from the ranks were often the

In a moment of quiet away from the rest of the raucous tavern scene from Hogarth's *A Rake's Progress* (1733), a pock-marked harlot slips her shoes over her laddered stockings. Beside her lie discarded stays, a heap of toppled pans and a suggestively skewered bird.

Far left: *The Beauty Unmask'd* (1770). While this could depict the literal unveiling of a woman dressed for a masquerade, it also hints at the popular anxiety about the concealment of corruption behind a façade. The mask motif is mirrored to grotesque effect in *Six Stages of Mending a Face* (page 30).

most revered. Nell Gwynne – self-proclaimed 'Protestant whore' of Charles II – received an affectionate tribute from writer Aphra Behn: 'you never appear but you glad[den] the hearts of all that have the happy fortune to see you, as if you were made on purpose to put the whole world into good humour.' Emma Hamilton, who married a British Ambassador and embarked on a notorious love affair with Horatio Nelson, also proved that those of humble beginnings could aspire to the *demi-monde*, entertain royalty or marry into wealth (although women such as Poll Forrester, whose less-than-delicate manners earned her the accolade 'drinks like a fish, eats like a horse, and swears like a trooper', would never have quite made the grade). Sarah Prydden (*c.* 1690/2–1724) achieved the first feat, but her career was blighted by her inability to act with propriety. An early biography suggests that the teenage Sarah (who was catapulted to fame as Sally Salisbury) was seduced by the iniquitous Colonel Charteris, and swept into the 'Pest-house' of Mother Wisebourne. By the time she reached twenty, London buzzed with news of her exploits; some of the more spurious rumours included her propensity for rolling old women down hills in barrels, and carousing with notorious street-gang the Mohocks

Left: The theatre was notoriously connected with 'seasonal' prostitution. Sophia Baddeley – here as Joan of Arc in 1774 – slipped comfortably into the life of a courtesan, but her fortunes fell and a decade later she appeared on the York stage 'stupidly intoxicated with Laudanum'.

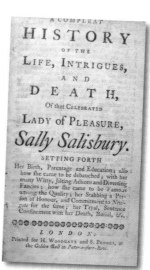

A COMPLEAT

HISTORY

OF THE

LIFE, INTRIGUES,

AND

DEATH,

Of that CELEBRATED

LADY of PLEASURE,

Sally Salisbury.

SETTING FORTH

Her Birth, Parentage and Education; also how she came to be debauched; with her many Witty, Jilting Actions and Diverting Fancies; how she came to be Famous among the Quality; her Stabbing a Person of Honour, and Commitment to New-gate for the same; her Tryal, Sentence Confinement with her Death, Burial, &c.

LONDON:

Printed for H. WOODGATE and S. BROOKS, at the Golden Ball in Pater-noster-Row.

The title page of an anonymous memoir of the life of Sally Salisbury. Noted women of pleasure – 'giants of mischief' such as Sally – fascinated society and inspired a profusion of biographies, bawdy songs and salacious prints.

The beautiful Emma Hamilton rose from lowly origins, reputedly beginning her career at a London brothel, to become England's most famous mistress. Renowned artists such as George Romney (who painted *Lady Hamilton as Circe* in about 1782) and Joshua Reynolds often found their muses in beautiful courtesans.

dressed in men's clothes (her true sex apparently not determined until a particularly thorough constable saw fit to rifle around in her breeches). As her inability to steady her temper worsened, Sally tumbled between lovers and lonely garrets, but her 'Great Catastrophe' came in 1722: in a fit of jealous rage, she stabbed a lover in the chest with a bread knife. She was committed to Newgate, where she died in 1724.

Some were renowned for their eccentricities – Kitty Fisher ate a banknote of 1,000 guineas on a slice of bread to prove that she could afford to be choosy about her clients – but others managed their affairs more prudently. Successful or ill-fated, their romances enthralled the public. After a notable career bedding politicians and princes, Elizabeth Armistead was happily married to Whig statesman Charles James Fox for many years. Actress Dorothea Jordan came to the attention of the Duke of Clarence in Catherine Windsor's bawdyhouse in 1790. Twenty years and ten illegitimate children later, she was discarded when the Duke discovered that he was to be proclaimed William IV. It was a lesson that many courtesans learned. Despite their prestigious conquests, the fortunes of Dorothea, Emma Hamilton, Harriette Wilson and the smallpox-scarred Nancy Jones – among many others – dwindled as their looks faded.

However, the majority of prostitutes simply sold their bodies to earn a wage. The reasons why women fell into the sex industry were hotly debated, and countless aspects of modern life – including the vanity encouraged by consumer culture, and even drinking tea – were identified as potential debauchers of youth. Particular trades were also perceived as 'preparatory schools for the brothel'. Defoe noted that badly paid servants had a tendency to slip 'into prostitution and back into service', and it was generally assumed that throwing a female street-seller a suggestive glance and a coin could buy more than ripe fruit. Dancers, singers and actresses struggling at the end of the theatrical season found ready money entertaining gentlemen in other ways. When women like Frances Abington began their stage careers 'exposing her lovely naked bosom to the gaze of lascivious leering gentlemen', it is unsurprising that lustful admirers sought them out after the curtain fell. Destitute women with no other means of income had little real alternative. Contemporary investigations revealed that many prostitutes were orphaned or abandoned at a young age. With no practical skills they had little chance of finding work, and the assurances of a kindly 'landlady' offering lodgings might appear very attractive. Those who had grown up in brothels simply knew no other world, and prostitution was considered the natural career path for girls such as Lucy Cooper and perhaps Nell Gwynne, who – according to Pepys – was a Madam's daughter, 'brought up in a bawdy-house to fill strong water to the guest[s].'

While fashionable whores strolled in parks and waited for clients to seek them out, 'bunters' were obliged to solicit on the streets, often threatened with violence if they failed to bring someone home. Many hunted in pairs or intimidating groups of six or seven to reduce personal danger and boost earnings. Money was the object: the pockets of a man insensible from liquor, or 'drunk in the Extasies of his Wicked Pleasure', were easily emptied by nimble fingers. Many whores actually considered this their primary vocation, preferring to view themselves as pickpockets simply using their bodies in order to better go about their business.

Below: Street-sellers were often targeted by leering gentlemen who expected that they could buy any common woman's favour. Here, a slightly dishevelled woman trundling along a barrowful of carrots is lewdly accosted by a passing gentleman (*Sandwich Carrots!*, 1796).

For the harlot – a woman whose earnings relied upon her appearance – costume and cosmetics were of singular importance. The bawd often provided suitable attire, and the prospect of silk skirts was irresistible to some impoverished girls. When William Morris spied a runaway servant in a Drury Lane brothel in 1734, he fumed to see her 'drest up, I'll warrnt ye, like one of the tip top Madams of the Hundreds.' Co-habiting women often shared their clothes and jewellery; in 1801, Jane Judd remarked that she and neighbouring lodgers 'lived in a state of prostitution, and used each others' apparel'.

Certain garments, colours and styles could signal the wearer's sexual availability. Beau Nash, Master of Ceremonies at Bath, appears to have considered white aprons as symbols of prostitution. In the 1790s, it was 'exceeding lascivious' to wear a nosegay of flowers 'on the left side of

THE MALE CARRIAGE

Sets out from Soho, at 8 o'clock in the Evening, stops at Drury Lane and Covent Garden to take in — inside Passengers to pay 1-1. — allowed to carry 2 &c. — the Carriage Heel springed, fresh painted, well guarded, and kept in good Order — the Axle-tree warranted from taking fire at the Motion be ever so quick. N.B. Places may be taken at the Sterling warehouse in the Garden, or of Mother Orange-chip in the Lobby.

This wonderfully cheeky depiction of a relatively fashionable 'Male Carriage' describes her thus: 'Sets out from Soho at 8 o'clock in the Evening, stops at Drury Lane and Covent Garden... the Carriage Heel springed, fresh painted, well guarded, and kept in good Order.' (1787)

[the] bosom; as high as the ear'. Purple gloves were worn by some to indicate special skills in flagellation. Of course, revealing clothes were the most crudely effective. *The Crafty Whore* (1658) described devious strumpets wearing pink satin with very short sleeves to accentuate the alluring whiteness of their skin. Some could only afford a single white ribbon, while others such as Samuel Taylor Coleridge's 'patched-up old Harlot' donned gaudy colours and encrusted themselves with precious stones and pearls before stepping out onto the cold night streets.

Gentlemen's mutterings about feminine beauty regimes grew increasingly anxious; an 'Act to protect men from being beguiled into marriage by false adornments' was even reportedly presented to Parliament in 1770. 'Paynted ladies' had for centuries been taken for common strumpets, and wenches of the Stuart era bedaubed their brows with so much powder that they 'glister[ed] like a Woodstreet Cake'. Unfortunately, they did not always get it right: one 'Miss Jo' used so much 'lamp-black and oil' to darken her hair that 'her head now stinks like a stale fishmongers shop.' In later decades, a natural ideal of beauty was pursued by whores and husband-hunters alike, leaving society fretting about how to distinguish between them. Girls entering the profession washed their faces with mercury water to keep it fair and lessen freckles, and avoided obvious cosmetics for as long as possible to maintain an air of youth and virtue.

However, Jonathan Swift's poem 'A Beautiful Young Nymph Going to Bed' (1732) exposed the hardened harlot's beauty regime as amounting to full-body reconstruction. Before retiring, 'Corinna' carefully picks out her crystal eye, removes her false hair, teeth, breasts and eyebrows, and applies ointment to her venereal sores. This repulsive spectacle emphasised that, sometimes, a painted face could barely disguise the rotting frame beneath.

The measures that the vast majority of prostitutes took to preserve their health were usually ineffective and often expensive. Venereal disease was something of an occupational hazard; prostitutes had been held accountable for the spread of syphilis – the 'French', 'Neapolitan' or 'English' disease, depending on where you cared to direct the blame – across Europe since the sixteenth century. The onset of this agonising – and as yet incurable – malady spelled trouble for the bawd and usually the end for the girl herself.

Bawdyhouse girls' experiences of medical matters varied according to the owner's wealth and inclinations. Charlotte Hayes made active attempts to ensure her employees' fitness for duty, with a Dr Chidwick performing regular health checks. Elsewhere, highly valued and mildly distempered whores, if they were fortunate, might be rested and treated in the house. Others were simply hidden away. The finger-pointing of tavern-owners privy to which girls had 'poison lurking in their veins' could seriously tarnish a brothel's reputation. In 1753, the *Derby Mercury* told of one 'hellish Hag' sending her infected employees upstairs 'into the Garret, to die by Inches, unpitied, and unrelieved.' The majority, however, would be cast out entirely, to 'pine out a diseased existence in some garret, or cellar.'

Many young whores would have been tempted into the profession by the fine clothes that a procuress could provide. In this print of 1750, an old bawd practically claps her hands with glee as she gazes upon the polished beauty she has created.

Naked except for ragged stockings, a whore washes her last remaining gown. Despite her elaborately ornamented hair, her professional success is belied by her humble lodgings, broken possessions and medicine bottles (James Gillray, *The Whore's Last Shift*, 1779).

Use of cosmetics was one of the feared 'wheedling arts' of Georgian women in general, and harlots in particular. Rowlandson's *Six Stages of Mending a Face* (1793) warned men that susceptibility to a pretty face could land them with an ugly crone for a wife or a diseased whore for a bedfellow.

SIX STAGES OF MENDING A FACE
~ dedicated with respect to the Right Hon.ble Lady Archer

Where treatment *was* sought, its effects could be as painful as the illness. A common treatment was 'salivation': mercury administered via pills, ointment or vapour baths. Only when 'the breath begins to stink, the gums to ake, the teeth to grow loose and stick out' were physicians advised to admit defeat. Quack cures for 'certain ailments' were peppered among newspaper advertisements, and most contemporary prints show the prostitute's household adorned with a medley of pots, pills and potions.

Prevention, of course, was preferable to cure. Condoms were increasingly widely available and their manufacture earned some, such as Teresia Constantia Phillips, a comfortable living. Many bawdyhouses were stocked with these 'machines', but there seems to have been confusion about whose responsibility they were; consumed by a sudden lust one night in 1762, James Boswell expected even a street-walking strumpet to provide the 'armour'.

Douches such as this one, dating from 1843, were mechanisms for maintaining cleanliness. In an unreliable and potentially dangerous method of birth control, the appliance could be filled with substances thought to prevent conception and pumped through a handling hose into the body.

Condoms acted as devices against disease, and early linen models were sometimes soaked in solutions of saline, vinegar or lemon juice as supposed spermicides. Their reliability is perhaps indicated by the fact that one manufacturer stipulated: 'for the sake of safety, two are advised to be worn'. Nevertheless, the popular assumption that prostitutes were rendered barren by their trade undoubtedly brought about unwanted pregnancies, and the physical and financial dangers of finding oneself with child could be life-threatening. Mother Needham flew to her 'Store-rais'd Closet of Gally-pots and Glasses' whenever her girls displayed tell-tale symptoms. Chemical concoctions thought to prevent conception were internally administered with douches, syringes and sponges, and products advertised as dangerous for pregnant women – such as 'Hooper's Female Pills' – were actively sought out by those already expecting. Mortality bills and pleas for support indicate that, where these abortions failed, abandonment and infanticide were a tragically common last resort.

Clearly, this catalogue of hazards and heartache did not make for an enviable life. Girls belonging to a brothel were bound by its rules, and bawds made escaping their clutches as difficult as possible. Absconders were often charged with the theft of clothes belonging to 'the house'. In 1735, Ann Mitchell was tried for stealing a gown, a nightgown and a smock: little more than the clothes on her back. Others were severely maltreated; when defending her 'theft' in 1812, Ann Middleton declared: 'she ill used me and beat me'. Those who *did* escape the bawdyhouse didn't necessarily renounce the life of prostitution entirely. With professional opportunities severely restricted for most women, while there was demand for sexual services, virtue continued to be overthrown.

Plate V of *A Harlot's Progress*. Moll lies insensible as physicians argue over her treatment. The medley of bottles and Dr Rock's venereal pills suggest that she has dabbled in popular quack remedies, and the fruit of her illegitimate pregnancy sits ignored on the floor.

THE MAN OF PLEASURE

IN MAY 1829, the *York Herald* reported that four young men had been arrested for disorderly behaviour, throwing stones and making 'tremendous noise' around Grape Lane. The rogues were apprehended making merry at a brothel in neighbouring Swinegate, and the reporter seems almost admiring in his description of them as 'dressed in the first style of fashion, one of them having mustachios.'

Even the libertines of the Restoration would have envied the teeming world of sexual pleasure available to the Georgian rake. The debauched culture of gentlemen's societies such as the Hellfire Club became legendary, and was increasingly an aspiration of the professional classes as well as the wealthy. Boisterous young gents inspired by their European travels imitated the pursuits of their elders; in 1817 Thomas Rowlandson summarised the life of the noble peer as 'divided between the brothel and the horse-course.' However, while mischievous youths were potentially open to eventual reform, the incurable lasciviousness and sexual fixations of others were ridiculed and reviled. In the early eighteenth century the aggressive sexual appetite of Colonel Charteris left society disgusted, and in later decades the lechery of the elderly Duke of Queensberry became a popular joke.

The brothel was the most direct way of indulging lustful passions, and just as their residents varied in refinement, so their clientele ranged from apprentices to princes. 'Polite society' sought out establishments such as Jane Goadby's for luxury inspired by the continent, or Charlotte Hayes's for exotic events. Military camps swarmed with prostitutes, and sailors sought relief from months at sea by spending their wages in the bawdyhouses of port towns. City stews were sought out by visiting country squires and their regular 'Brothel-Haunters', many of whom made little attempt to conceal their business. In 1752, Philip Church answered accusations about his keeping a brothel by casting aspersions on a neighbouring tavern, and when asked for evidence, boldly replied: 'I am there every Night myself with a Whore, and I thank G— I can afford it.' In any case, whoring had its advantages over taking a wife; in 1774, one writer cheekily declared that it was the only way

Opposite: Despite the ominous sign, 'Men traps are laid here every night', a knowing advertisement for 'Dr Leak's Pills', and a sinister-looking door knocker, an eager young rake looks hungrily up at the women of Mrs Mitchell's establishment in Cleveland Row (*Charity Covereth a Multitude of Sins*, 1781)

William Douglas, the 4th Duke of Queensberry (1724/5–1810), or 'Old Q', was a widely ridiculed and incurably lecherous eccentric of the late eighteenth century. In this print of 1795, his hands are firmly stuck down his breeches, presumably as he ogles alluring young women.

Far right: Colonel Francis Charteris (1675–1732), a notorious 'terror to female innocence'. In Plate I of A Harlot's Progress, he looks on lasciviously as a young virgin is procured for him. He was convicted of forcing himself on a maidservant in 1730, and became known as the 'Rape-Master General of Britain'.

A poor man loaded with mischief, or matrimony (1752) is a comical view of marriage, almost encouraging men into whoredom. Chained to his gin-soaked sot of a wife, this unfortunate fellow stumbles past a building bearing the horns of the cuckold.

to avoid 'the pukings, longings, and peevish importunities' of a 'breeding woman'. Not that marriage was really any impediment to illicit dalliances, as many wives found to their despair.

Nevertheless, whoring was a notoriously dangerous sport and promiscuity could lead a man to his ruin. Pamphlets purporting to reveal the 'arts of the harlot' warned how they could 'intice with gestures, nodds, amorous and petulant glances' (authors invariably balanced their sage advice with semi-pornographic narratives, presumably leaving the conflicted reader at once fired with anxiety and sexual arousal). The Miss Display'd (1675) absolved men of all responsibility by proclaiming that they 'differ[ed] not from a beast... having the same brutish appetites'. This inherent inability to resist womanly wiles drove them to distraction. In the 1750s one anonymous pamphlet complained that even coffeehouse owners employed 'ogling, pretty, young Hussies to be our Bar-keepers, steal away our Hearts, and insensibly betray us to Extravagance.'

In The Orphan, playwright Thomas Otway warned: 'Keep thy

A young woman discovers her beau leaving a 'Temple of Venus'. Many employees of such establishments were well versed in refusing admittance to angry wives in search of roving husbands. One lady, demanding entry to Haddock's Bagnio in 1752, was told that her spouse 'had a Lady with him and should not be disturb'd'.

Eyes from wand'ring, Man of Frailty: Beware the dang'rous Beauty of the Wanton … Ruin like a Vulture Waits on their Steps.' This ruin might be moral, physical or financial, and was sometimes absolute. In 1725, an elderly basket-seller was discovered dead in a brothel on the Strand, 'drowned in an excessive quantity of *Strip-and-go-naked*, alias, *Strike Fire*, alias, *Gin*'. In 1791, two naval officers were murdered in a bawdyhouse in Portsmouth, 'and from thence dragged to the embrazures on the beach.' In 1819, the *Hereford Journal* reported a killing in 'one of the infamous brothels in Dover-Street' as if their heartlessness was to be expected; inviting an ill-fated pie salesman into their house, the wretches stole his pies and 'hooted and laughed at him' before striking him to death with pots and a poker.

Even those venturing on to safer establishments did not always leave untainted. The risk of venereal disease was ever-present, and its physical effects destroyed a man's reputation. Referring to the terrible ravages of syphilis, in 1750 Lord Chesterfield advised his son that 'a man may lose his heart with dignity; but if he loses his nose, he loses his character into the bargain.' There does, however,

Slumped in the 'Stool of Repentance', a fragile, boil-covered man holds his head and vomits into a pot. Various medications, and some of his teeth, lie on a table next to him. Through his suffering he murmurs: 'No more Wives, or Mercury, dear Doctor!' (*The Polygamist*, 1781.)

When not chronicling the witticisms of his friend Dr Johnson, James Boswell (1740–95) recorded his own life and sexual conquests. After barely resisting a common strumpet because neither had 'armour', he later 'trembled at the danger I had escaped'.

Quack doctors of the period profited greatly from the desperation of those infected with venereal disease, and miracle cures for 'a certain disease' littered popular newspapers (*The Apothecary's Hall*, 1814).

seem to have been something of a community of sufferers, most openly in the establishment of the 'No-Nos'd Club' in London, where indefatigable chronicler of city life Ned Ward observed a 'Fashion of flat faces' in 1709.

In the folly of youth, some gloried in the number of minor illnesses they had contracted, as a testament to their sexual prowess. This bravado is even more mystifying considering the treatments they had to endure. William Hickey's experience of mercury poisoning was excruciating: 'my head suddenly swelled to an enormous size, my tongue and mouth became so inflamed that I could take no other nourishment than liquids.' Understandably, in the first instance most sought a cure in popular quack remedies. One mid-century medicine supposedly suited to hot chocolate would have been particularly appealing, not least because it presented a cunning way of secretly dosing wives who had also been unwittingly infected by their husband's infidelity. Although others hoped to be cured by 'taking the waters' at Bath spa, the sexual temptations patently on offer undoubtedly defeated the object of many medicinal excursions.

But even when taking precautions against disease, a bawdyhouse client was vulnerable in other ways. Inebriated punters were targeted by their contemporaries (in 1738 one man's drinking partner feebly protested: 'the Man had got drunk, and I took his Money out of his Pocket, in order to take Care of it for him…'), and most of the prostitutes appearing in court stood accused of theft. Some were experts in their field: in 1801, Thomas Harris awoke to find that his valuables had disappeared even after taking the care to wrap them in his breeches and use them as a pillow. Other women were less shrewd. Mary Loyd's trial in 1735 came about after her boasts to a full tavern: 'I took my Opportunity, and stript the Rascal naked.' Some bawdyhouse robberies required elaborate teamwork, and a well-timed intrusion by an apparently enraged house bully could throw clients into such confusion that they momentarily lost all consideration for the contents of their pockets.

Any man with accusations was promptly expelled from the building by the bawd or a bully, and extreme violence was not unusual. One man robbed in a Norwich brothel in 1742 later sent his servant to reiterate his demands for compensation; not only was he again refused, but a house ruffian chased the servant down the street and cut his throat. Men hoping to escape their half of the 'pleasure first, pay later' bargain found themselves similarly abused. Even those taking their grievances to higher powers were not always remunerated. When Andrew Hill was robbed of £65 in a brothel in Newgate, York in 1829, the court simply admonished him for allowing himself to be defrauded in this way on such a regular basis and requested that he be sober at the next hearing.

Stains on a man of quality's reputation were harder to dismiss than holes in his pocket. For one thing, courtesans could afford to be choosy. When Casanova suffered a rebuff, he sought revenge by teaching his pet parrot to squawk 'Miss Charpillon is a greater whore than her mother' (his target's complete indifference only riled him further). Worse than damaged pride was public ridicule. When a courtesan's fortunes began to wane, many published their memoirs as a means of raising cash – not only from sales revenue, but through blackmailing former lovers. The 'autobiography' of Regency beauty Harriette Wilson is perhaps the most famous, not least because her attempts to threaten the Duke of Wellington met with a sharp and unprecedented response: 'Publish, and be damned!' Needless to say, he was mocked ruthlessly throughout.

Many felt safer procuring a wench with the help of a bawd, or the 'waiter-pimps' who brought willing parties together in taverns. In theory, these middlemen would avoid those they knew were 'pox'd', but exemplar of the trade Jack Harris revealed that 'by pimp, nothing more was signified than to run about the neighbourhood and bring the first bunter to the gentleman'.

This early nineteenth-century condom was fashioned from sheep gut soaked in water and 'bordered at the open end with a riband'. Earlier models were made of linen, silk or leather. Other methods of contraception were also employed; in an experimental mood, Casanova persuaded one unfortunate lover to use half a lemon rind as a cervical cap.

The Duke of Wellington was ridiculed repeatedly in the memoirs of Regency courtesan Harriette Wilson. Here, she leaves him outside her door, with 'rain trickling down his nose, his voice, trembling with rage and impatience', while she entertained another lover, the Duke of Argyll (*The General Out-Generalled*, 1808).

Harris perhaps had more flair for the job than his contemporaries, and it was he who lent his name to *Harris' List*, which quickly became an essential purchase for the man of pleasure and sold over 250,000 copies. Light-hearted but erotic, these pocketbooks listed the addresses, attributes, skills and history of local whores, and identified those to avoid. A particularly bad review fell to Lucy P–terson in 1761: 'in a homely phrase, a vile bitch', and an edition of 1791 warned of Miss Nunn, a girl so lusty that she once bit off part of a man's tongue. It revealed where to satisfy unusual desires – Eliza Love was a 'd—d fine hairy piece' (1789), and the obese Miss Jordan had 'a face somewhat resembling a full moon' (1779) – and offered tips for seducing particular women. Chillingly, the reluctant whore Hannah Dalton was reportedly 'most agreeable when half-drunk' (1761).

A visitor's experience of a bawdyhouse varied according to its rules and conventions. Some were led into a chamber adorned with pornographic artworks, 'Intermixt with the Pictures of Ladies of Pleasure'. After indicating his preference, he was escorted to her room. A visitor to Mrs Goadby's establishment recounts that guests drank, danced and supped freely with its residents. If a woman accepted a silk handkerchief from a suitor, they would spend the night together. Mother Douglas employed uniformed footmen to present visitors with beribboned condoms before conducting them upstairs. Of course, other liaisons were less fanciful. On Richard Perry's visit to a low brothel, Mary Aldridge led him upstairs, a woman 'came up for money for the room, I paid her, she went out, and I lock'd the door.'

Of course, some customers were not seeking complete sexual gratification. Theresa Berkeley explained that many of the elderly men visiting her whipping parlour did so because it 'keeps up a little agreeable excitement in their systems long after the power of enjoying the opposite sex has failed them.' After being approached by two street-walkers in 1725, Joseph Richmond admitted paying them 'not to do them over, but for them to strip naked, and show me some Tricks.' Not saving his blushes, they attested that he then requested they fetch some rods, to 'make us good Girls; and then for us to whip him to make him a good Boy'. Darling of the voyeur, Restoration harlot Priss Carsewell invited curious gentlemen to play 'chucking', a game requiring her to stand on her head while they threw half-crowns 'into her Commodité'. Interestingly, London records turn up the occasional brothel frequented by 'lady-clients'. At one establishment, lustful women peeped through windows on the doors of men's rooms and informed the chambermaid of their choice. No doubt these women would have been viewed quite differently from male 'brothel-haunters' if discovered, and they were certainly required to pay more handsomely for the privilege.

Frontispiece to the 1794 edition of *Harris' List*, the man of pleasure's essential pocketbook. Here, clutching his copy, a man looks eagerly into the house of 'Miss Love' while two wanton women beckon out of the windows.

This print of a seventeenth-century bawdyhouse illustrates the means by which many brothels advertised the wares of their establishment, whereby visiting clients viewed the portraits of each girl and indicated their preferences.

BEYOND THE BAWDYHOUSE

T HE BUSINESS OF PROSTITUTION was, of course, by no means confined within the walls of the bawdyhouse. Even those belonging to a brothel were part of a much wider culture of selling sex, which – although most visible in urban life – was woven into the nation's fabric, much to the dismay of its moralists. England's streets, taverns, parks, theatres – even its churches – crawled with women hoping to sell their bodies.

In 1788, an inquiry into prostitution concluded that 'none of the human Species are more miserable in themselves, or more mischievous in Society, than those Unhappy Women, who disgrace our Streets.' As we have seen, street-walking was a necessary part of the trade for girls belonging to lower-class establishments, but others worked independently, perhaps simply hoping to earn enough for a night's lodging. For many, prostitution acted as an occasional supplement to income. In 1809, Elizabeth Perry insisted: 'I have two small children; my husband is out of employ and a cripple; I went out that night to get a shilling by prostitution.' Most were not particularly sophisticated in their attempts to attract attention. Describing his encounter with Sarah Oakley in 1732, Richard Trigtoe stated: 'up comes the Prisoner and says to me, How do you do? Why, pretty well, says I. Won't you come and see my Lodgings? Says she.' In 1726, Defoe bemoaned the 'Twitches on the Sleeve', 'ogling Salutations' and 'insolent Demands of Wine and Treats' that inevitably intruded upon his evening walks.

However, not all men were quite so impervious to their entreaties, and once willing parties had reached an agreement, the final matter to resolve was the location of the act. As we have seen, taverns, bagnios and landlords were often willing to turn a blind eye to paying 'Single men and their Wives', and on one occasion Boswell simply gratified his lusts on Westminster Bridge, remarking 'the whim of doing it there with the Thames rolling below us amused me much.' However, it seems that finding a suitable spot wasn't always so simple. In 1727, a Thames waterman was forced – at the point of a sword – to row a lusty gentleman and his companion to Chelsea Reach so that he could 'occupy' her in the boat. The waterman was so disgusted that he later burned his boat to ashes.

Opposite:
Vauxhall Pleasure Gardens first opened to the public in 1661 and quickly became notorious for allowing the worlds of fashion and fornication to collide effortlessly, with 'no idea of elegance or propriety' (print by Rowlandson, 1784).

Disreputable women were usually to be met with at public taverns, particularly if the establishment lent out their rooms to couples without asking questions. Some city taverns even employed 'waiter-pimps' who, in the absence of a bawd, could find eager gents a willing companion.

A Trip to Cocks Heath (1778). This suggestive image follows a gaggle of bedraggled military officers and their female companions heading towards the army camp at Coxheath. Ahead of them, three women examine a phallic-looking cannon.

Opportunities for sexual gratification lurked in the shadows of all places affiliated with pleasure and entertainment. Theatre districts came alive with the opening of the season, and the stage, the audience pit, and the expensive opera box allowed women with varying pretensions to gentility to advertise their availability or distribute their favours. The 'Outrageous and flaming Debauchery' to be found at the increasingly

fashionable masquerades – such as those at Teresa Conelys' 'fairy palace' in Soho Square – allowed for anonymous encounters, where masked whores mixed freely with the nation's notables.

Bagnios, although perceived as thinly disguised brothels, were often managed quite differently. Some self-promoted brazenly in the newspapers, claiming to be 'open every Hour in the Year… for both Rich and Poor' or 'Accommodated with handsome lodgings to lye all Night'. The provision of girls also tended to be arranged differently in bath-houses; one foreign visitor observed that 'Girls do not live here, but they are fetched in [sedan] chairs when required', also noting 'the business of such a house is conducted with a seriousness and propriety which is hard to credit.'

Astute bawds encouraged their charges to work their charms wherever they could, knowing that the best way to attract custom was publicity. Helpfully, newspapers were always eager to report where these Matrons 'and their Meretricious Attendants' had been observed promenading, or showing off their carriages. When the theatrical season ended and custom grew thinner, many 'exercised' (or flaunted) their girls in the pleasure gardens, but since many admitted anyone with a shilling, the wares on offer were by no means exclusive. Some were content simply to broadcast their beauty; on a stroll through St James's Park, Boswell spied 'one in a red cloak of a good buxom person and comely face whom I marked out as a future piece'. Others were ready to complete the transaction there and then – or at least

Above left:
The pits and stalls of theatres offered ample opportunity for amorous encounters. In Hogarth's The Laughing Audience (1733), those engrossed in the play are oblivious to the attempted seductions taking place in the theatre box behind them.

Above:
Courtesans also took every opportunity to advertise their beauty by hiring prominent theatre and opera boxes and waiting for gentlemen to beg an audience with them (A Side Box, 1781).

Right: *Dressing for a Masquerade* (1790). Four wenches transformed into anonymous nymphs in preparation for a masquerade. In 1754, the *Gentleman's Magazine* considered these events the worst example of 'the wantonness of luxury that has of late [been] introduced into the kingdom'.

professed to be, to the annoyance of one friend of Casanova's: 'I offered her twenty guineas if she would come and take a little walk with me in a dark alley.' After demanding the money in advance, the adventuress deserted him as soon as they found themselves alone.

Outings to surrounding towns were organised with an eye to self-promotion. In 1773, Mother Mitchell took a coach-load of excited girls to Oxford for the Encaenia festivities, where they drew considerable attention to themselves by splashing each other provocatively in the river, crying 'Lord have mercy, my bubbies!' The nymphs of Mother Windsor's establishment graced Brighton and Bath with their presence. Writing to a friend in 1750, the radical politician John Wilkes advised: 'If you prefer young women and whores to old women and wives ... hasten to town to take a place in my post-chaise to Bath.'

Brothel girls could be hired out for special occasions, and bawds granting favours for prestigious clients were amply rewarded. Gentlemen's clubs and sex societies occasionally applied to local brothel-keepers

Right: Bagnios offering 'neat lodgings for men' were viewed as little more than brothels, and were a common resort of adulterous couples looking for a place to conduct their 'criminal conversations' (*Retail traders not affected by the shop tax*, 1787).

for supplies of women to entertain them, whether naked dancers or something more intimate. The Beggar's Benison Club in the Scottish fishing village of Anstruther (whose motto was 'May prick nor purse ne'er fail you') offered bawds legal and social freedoms within their 'commonwealth' in return.

Professional whoredom was, of course, a full-time occupation. Mother Wisebourne even encouraged her girls to tout for custom when they went to church. An employee recalled that: 'We'd take all opportunities ... to lift up our coats so high, that we might shew our handsome legs and feet ... by which means the gallants would be sure either to dog us themselves, or else to send their footmen to see where we liv'd.'

Inevitably, such audacity invited criticism from conservative quarters. Society at large held manipulative bawds and wicked debauchers in contempt, but there were conflicting views about how the girls themselves should be treated. With the nation so divided over the social and moral problems posed by prostitution, the debate generated an equally irreconcilable range of solutions, from the sympathetic to the uncompromisingly ruthless.

Many bawdyhouses hired out their girls to paying customers. Clutching glasses of wine and losing their academic caps, a group of rakish Oxford University undergraduates seize hold of their chance to smuggle a woman into their college (*An Old Varsity Trick* by Thomas Rowlandson).

As this print suggests, Georgian Bath was equally renowned as a place to restore health and admire beautiful women. The Parades, the Assembly Rooms and the Baths themselves were popular haunts of prostitutes hoping to ensnare fashionable young roués (*A View of the Parade at Bath*, c. 1780s).

PUNISH OR PROTECT?

IN 1703, author John Dunton took it upon himself to solve the problem of prostitution, and he began prowling the streets of London, following wanton women around and loudly reciting Biblical verse in their direction. Although his efforts didn't produce the wave of repentance he had imagined, he thought the exercise worthwhile, if only for the glow of self-satisfaction it gave *him*.

His voice was one among thousands offering answers to a provocative question that would grow more urgent over the coming decades. Those raging that lost virtue was irrecoverable saw tolerance of prostitution only as encouragement to vice, and called for the infestation to be eradicated by 'the Whipping-Post, Work-House and Transportation'. From mid-century, however, the growing conviction that fallen women were victims of circumstance, rather than inherently sinful, mobilised support for the establishment of penitentiaries aiming to 'reclaim' them. The prostitute's treatment at the hands of the law, charitable reformers, and her neighbours revolved around one key issue: did she deserve punishment or protection?

Being branded a 'disorderly house' usually sounded the death knell for a common stew, but opinion differed on whether brothels were *generally* considered a public nuisance. They were certainly viewed as such by the Society for the Reformation of Manners (formed in 1691), which aimed to suppress all immorality in London, and named the worst offenders. By the publication of their seventh 'Black List' in 1702, members claimed to have brought 5,646 'keepers of houses of bawdry [or] whores, night-walkers, &c' to justice. Seventy years later, however, the *Morning Chronicle* complained that the midnight riots in the brothels of Long Acre were still 'a continual terror to the sober part of the neighbourhood'. When an Englishman was imprisoned for stirring up a riot in a Parisian brothel in 1768, it was said that he did so 'in the true English taste.' Occasionally, neighbours felt obliged to intervene: in 1762, when the cry of 'Murder!' was heard in one of the brothels in Tower Lane, Bristol, concerned locals 'applied to proper Officers and searched the House.'

Opposite:
Plate IV of A
Harlot's Progress.
Moll serves her
sentence in
Bridewell Prison.
As she beats hemp,
a prison guard
primes himself to
strike her if she
falters, as a
winking hag fingers
her fine clothes.

Under the supervision of local constables, night watchmen patrolled the streets between 9 p.m. and sunrise, conveying suspicious characters to the watchhouse. Initially an unpaid post that all male householders were expected to fill at some point, as the policing system developed, the majority of London watchmen were salaried by 1800.

WATCHMAN

Right: Constructed in 1793 and later restored, this sentry box silently surveys Norfolk Crescent in Bath. Stone structures became more common during Queen Anne's reign, as the watchmen inhabiting the wooden models grew tired of being tipped over by drunken rogues looking to entertain themselves.

Far right: As an old night watchman yawns he fails to notice two young harlots brazenly sweet-talking a naïve country squire while they pick his pockets (*A Cake in Danger*, c. 1806).

Although a statute against brothel-keeping was proclaimed in 1752, it was not properly enforced until over a century later. In 1811, the *Hereford Journal* complained that: 'the shameless conduct of the lower order of Prostitutes in this city, has long been a disgrace to its police.' In any case, houses with influential patrons escaped real punishment, and even the lowest could be excused if neighbours lent their support. This ill-defined legal position was easily exploited; in 1820 a number of brazen Madams even dared to take clients to court for attempting to pay with forged bank notes.

Bawds routinely used aliases and gave false addresses in an attempt to evade the authorities, but suspected houses of ill repute were closely observed by local beadles and night watchmen. When threatened, most were quick to defend themselves. Prints of bawdyhouse raids habitually depict enraged whores guarding their homes and brandishing various household weapons, or welcoming the unfortunate intruders with the contents of their chamberpots.

Chaos reigns as a man is trampled beneath the feet of a prostitute defending her home. She fixes her steely gaze on a group of marauders at her door, raising a stick threateningly at them, while her colleagues brandish furniture and their clients' swords (*The Guards of the Night Defeated*, 1774).

Those found guilty of 'receiving and entertaining lewd and disorderly persons, whoring and misbehaving themselves' could be punished by a spell in the pillory, fined or imprisoned. In 1719, brothel-keeper Mary Terry suffered the former, and was showered with rotten eggs and dirt. For some this amounted to the death sentence; following her conviction in 1731, Mother Needham died of her injuries after being severely pelted in the pillory by a disgusted public. The severity of their sentence depended on the perceived depravity of their crimes. In 1823, Jane Bray of The Lion and Anchor in Exeter was simply charged £5 and costs for keeping disorderly houses, but in Edinburgh in 1737, a bawd named Mrs McNab was 'drummed thro' the City, the Hangman walking behind her, and sent to the House of Correction for three years' after having been found responsible for the debauching of a young girl.

Although prostitution did not contravene any actual legislation, whores were also brought to account if they behaved in a 'disorderly' manner. Flogging, the Biblical punishment for those guilty of sexual misdemeanours, was still considered appropriate, often with the stipulation that blood must be drawn. The punishment was carried out in public and the offender whipped 'through the Streets, having the Outsides polluted with Mire and Filth, as a just Emblem of their polluted Insides'. In 1725, Eleanor Knight was 'order'd to be whip'd at the Cart's Tail from Brentford Bridge to the Market Place there on a Market Day, until her body were bloody.' Many were stripped to the waist, perhaps partly explaining writer Ned Ward's assertion that gangs of men made excursions to witness whores being flogged as a matter of entertainment.

Repeat offenders, or those discovered in particularly indecent situations, were more likely to be incarcerated – a sentence that could, at a stroke, ruin the girl's life and devastate the house to which she belonged. It must have been a blow to the manager of a 'brothel of note' in Marsh Street, Bristol, when six of her ladies were imprisoned in 1767. Despite the enforced physical labour and terrible living conditions in Georgian houses of correction, reformer Saunders Welch argued that they were 'little better than nurseries of debauchery'. Visiting Bridewell Prison in the 1720s, César de Saussure was shocked to see women in finery beating hemp alongside wretches in rags. Appearing to be a lady of quality was clearly worthless: '[the inspector] held a long cane in his hand about the thickness of my little finger, and whenever one of these ladies was fatigued and ceased working he would rap them on the arms, and in no gentle fashion, I can tell you.'

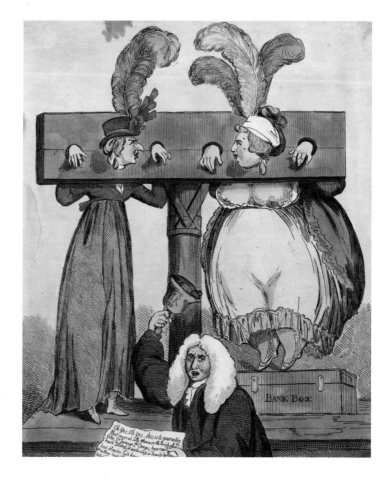

These ladies – members of the 'Faro' club of female gamblers – are suffering a stint in the pillory for their sinful ways. Many whores and bawds suffered the same humiliating fate, which could prove fatal if they attracted a hostile crowd (*Cocking the Greeks*, 1796).

Popular justice was also meted out by disapproving neighbours or unruly mobs, and, as with the riots of 1668, hostility occasionally translated into violence. Some protesters called themselves defenders of virtue, some were animated by political doctrine, others simply sought personal revenge, but all could be terribly destructive. In 1791, Fleet Lane – an area of Dublin 'infamous for its numerous receptacles of the lowest prostitutes and most desperate villains' – was targeted by a large mob seeking revenge for an assault made on a soldier by a bully. Ransacking of brothels along the Strand in July 1749 was initiated by a handful of demobilised sailors robbed by bullies employed by a bawdyhouse known as The Star. Returning supported by a crowd reportedly four hundred strong, they 'cut the feather-beds to pieces' and turned the women naked outdoors, before smashing windows and reveling in the success of their moral crusade.

Public humiliation was a softer disciplinary measure. In Francis Grose's *Slang Dictionary* (1811), 'docking' was the usual punishment for a prostitute responsible for infecting a sailor with venereal disease: the unfortunate

The 'Ducking Stool' – called the 'joy and terror of the town' by poet Benjamin West – had not only been used to punish those guilty of prostitution, but also brawling wives, cussing women and suspected witches. This print of 1819 depicts the practice in Daub Holes Field, Manchester.

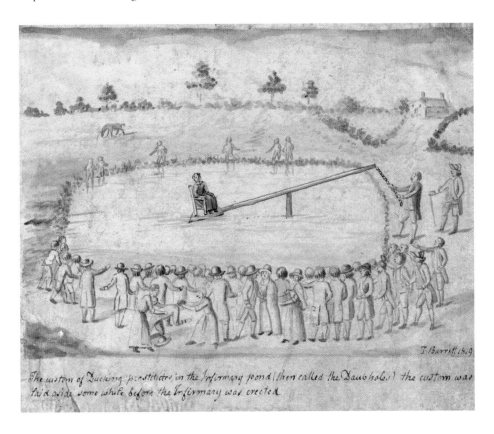

The custom of Ducking prostitutes in the Infirmary pond (then called the Daub holes) the custom was laid aside some while before the Infirmary was erected

T. Barritt 1819

Bridewell.

A *Prospect of Bridewell Prison* from the early eighteenth century. Those deemed to be vagrants or 'idle persons' by local beadles frequently found themselves swept through its doors, and whores numbered highly among them.

hussy would be turned out into the street in only her stays. Community shaming rituals to punish sexual aberrations such as adultery or cuckoldom were inevitably inspired and coloured by the dalliances of prostitutes and married men, or married women selling their favours. Whispers about 'criminal conversations' (adulterous acts) could develop into organised demonstrations of disapproval known as charivari or 'rough music', with crowds assembling outside the offenders' houses clanging pots and pans. In rural rituals known as 'Skimmington rides', or 'riding the stang' in the north, the humiliated husband of a loose woman might be paraded in drag through the streets on the back of a donkey.

However, less troublesome harlots were tolerated by their neighbours, and arrests were even impeded by protective locals. When four 'women of the town' were apprehended in London in 1730, a party of passing men leapt to their assistance, 'beat[ing] the watch and Constables to such a degree that they were obliged to release them.' Occasionally, the law even favoured the rights of the bawdyhouse over its own representatives: in 1729 a constable was punished for ransacking brothels without legal authority and blackmailing the bawds in return for 'his pretended Civility in not taking away their Creatures.'

As charitable sentiment towards the impoverished, the diseased, illegitimate children and fallen women gained momentum, it was physically manifested in the asylums built to treat and rehabilitate them. Instead of relying on parish relief or living in the shadow of the local workhouse, new doors opened to prostitutes with the foundation of a number of benevolent institutions. The first Lock Hospital, for those infected with venereal disease, opened in London in 1747. Those admitted were offered one chance at rehabilitation – once they were discharged as 'cured', they could not be readmitted. The Foundling Hospital, opened in 1749, took in unwanted infants, thereby offering both women and illegitimate children a chance at a new life.

Thomas Coram (c. 1668–1751). A former naval officer, Coram established London's Foundling Hospital after years of tireless campaigning. Despite good intentions, its admission of unwanted infants was seen by many critics as an encouragement to illicit sexual activity.

A penitent prostitute stands outside the Magdalen Hospital (from William Dodd's An Account of the Rise, Progress and Present State of the Magdalen Hospital, 1776).

Magdalene Hospitals, or 'Penitentiaries for Fallen Women', appeared around the country from the 1750s. In 1822, a letter to the Yorkshire Gazette jealously eyed the hospital at Hull, an exemplary model 'far exceeding' those already at Edinburgh, Liverpool and Bath. After extensive religious instruction, the sufficiently repentant were found 'creditable situations' and reintroduced into society. The isolated and rigorous daily regime enforced in these early institutions mirrored those of prisons, or monasteries, more closely than our modern idea of 'hospitals'. In 1820 a report into the sixty-year career of the London Magdalen Hospital ran thus: 'There have been 4,829 young women admitted into it, of whom 3,236 have been restored to habits of virtuous industry.' Less commendably, 103 'became lunatic' and 563 were 'discharged for improper behaviour'. Regardless of the accuracy of these statistics, and despite the rumblings of moral discontent they raised, many women regarded the Magdalene Hospitals as their only hope of salvation.

CONCLUSION

In 1630, a poem entitled 'The Virtuous Bawd' described the business of managing a house of ill fame as 'not some upstart newfangled *bauble* or *toy* ... but a real solid lasting thing.' The history of the brothel was certainly long if not exactly illustrious. During the Georgian era, the 'Misteries of the Bawdyhouse' were viewed by some outsiders with curiosity and amusement, and even those condemning them as nests of infamy could not agree whether the virtue of their residents still glimmered bleakly or if it had flickered and died the moment they had surrendered their bodies to 'pleasure'. Irrespective of the various romantic or diabolic notions of bawdyhouses – whether they symbolised the expression of natural passions or the earthly manifestation of 'Satan's Regiments' – they were at the heart of what was, essentially, a means of survival for women who would otherwise have faced destitution. The majority of prostitutes – and even bawds, although contemporaries would never have entertained the idea – were compelled into the trade by necessity, not inclination. In 1740, brothel-keeper Elizabeth Carter simply stated: 'My husband's a shoemaker, and I have a Child to Nurse, and do what I can to keep the Wolf from the Door.'

Detail from Rowlandson's print of Vauxhall, depicting the young Prince of Wales whispering sweet nothings to actress and royal mistress Mary 'Perdita' Robinson.

Selling sex may not have been invented in the Georgian era, but the permissive society that reigned in the 'long' eighteenth century allowed for new, exciting, and more public sexual encounters. As the Victorian era dawned, God-fearing moral crusades, anxiety about disease, and the relegation of promiscuous women once more to the status of 'social menace' encouraged an unnerved public to take a resolved stance against prostitution. This unsympathetic discourse not only suffocated the infant campaigns to 'rescue' the fallen woman, but strapped the formerly fashionable heaving bosom into a strait-laced Victorian corset and banished the open business of pleasure firmly to the past.